D0990215

Morris County MEMORIES

THE LATER YEARS ~ 1940-1969

ACKNOWLEDGMENTS

The *Daily Record* is pleased to present "Morris County Memories: Volume II." We have once again had the pleasure of working with people and organizations from throughout the county to produce this unique pictorial book covering the 1940s, '50s and '60s. It is only through their generous contribution of time and rich photo archives that this book is possible.

All Morris County residents are indebted to the many individuals from these organizations who are committed to preserving our history in libraries, historical societies, museums, archives and personal collections. We thank them for their dedication.

The following organizations have contributed to
"Morris County Memories: Volume II ~ The 1940s, '50s and '60s"

Denville Historical Society and Museum

Historical Society of the Township of Chatham

Lake Hopatcong Historical Society

Madison Historical Society

Madison Public Library

Morris County Historical Society

Morris Plains Museum

Morristown/Morris Township Free Public Library

Mt. Olive Township Historical Society

Parsippany Historical and Preservation Society

Picatinny Arsenal

Roxbury Township Historical Society

Whippany Railway Museum

TABLE OF CONTENTS

FOREWORD

Every year is important, but the 30 years from 1940 to 1969 are the backbone of today's Morris County. In those three decades our population increased a whopping 205 percent. Nearly 250,000 people joined the 125,000 already here. The fastest-growing decade? The Fifties, when the population grew nearly 60 percent. There were nearly 100,000 more people in Morris County at the end of the decade than there were at the beginning. Compare that to the recently-ended 1990s, when the population grew just 11.6 percent to reach 470,212.

This great post-war boom brought dozens of big businesses to Morris County. Some followed the lead of the Warner-Lambert Co. (which was merged into Pfizer in 2000) – it moved its headquarters here (from Brooklyn to Morris Plains) in 1947. Others followed in a great buildup that turned Morris County into one the nation's most influential and affluent centers of business ... and a great place to live, work and play.

The Daily Record has recorded, and often mirrored, that growth every day since 1900. We were there in 1942 when the first Morris Countians went off to World War II. We were there in 1959 when the Port Authority of New York announced plans to build an airport in the Great Swamp. We were there in 1969 when some well-dressed women stopped, for a while, bulldozers bringing Route 287 ("the new Route 202") through Morristown.

We're here today, too, bringing you stories we never would have believed in ways we would never have imagined. Who would have foreseen the Internet in 1940, for instance, or reading the news on www.dailyrecord.com?

Bringing you the news and serving our advertisers has been our passion for more than 100 years. We hope you enjoy Morris County Memories, the Later Years.

Walt T. Lafferty
President and Publisher
Daily Record

VIEWS AROUND THE COUNTY

These were the years when Morris County came of age. At the start of World War II, some of the great hotels on Lake Hopatcong, once reached by rail and steamboat, were still running, although they were about to disappear. In photographs, the downtowns – Denville, Dover, Morris Plains, Madison – look quaint and, well, old. The cars are dead giveaways. There are no Routes 80 and 287, although they were just around the corner. Instead, there is a relatively open-looking Route 10, once the site of an Indian path and in the late '40s looking like a superhighway.

Chester, the town of antiques, looks nearly unchanged. The Bertrand Island Amusement Park was in its heyday, 50-some years before a developer would begin building townhouses there. Streets were uncrowded, looking like something out of the "Twilight Zone."

This was about to change. The war was followed by an unimaginable boom that more than tripled Morris County's population between 1940 and 1969, exchanged farms and open spaces with homes, office parks and corporate headquarters, and crossed the county with important, north-south, east-west interstate highways. Morris County was about to become the fastest growing place in New Jersey, a heavyweight center for the nation's leading businesses and one of the more fashionable places to live and work in the United States.

Hotels on Lake Hopatcong, circa 1955. *Courtesy of Lake Hopatcong Historical Museum*

Blackwell Street, Dover, 1940s. *Courtesy of Joan S. Case*

Main Street, looking west, Chester, 1940s. *Courtesy Joan S. Case*

Main Street in Netcong, circa 1950. *Courtesy of Thea Dunkle, Mt. Olive Township Historical Society*

John Ehrhart looking down at Waverly Place from railroad overpass, Madison, 1940s. *Courtesy of Madison Public Library*

Aerial view
of Denville,
August 2,
1949. *Courtesy of*
Denville
Historical Society
and Museum

Business section, Long Valley, circa 1950. *Courtesy of Thea Dunkle, Mt. Olive Township Historical Society*

Meyersville Road after construction, 1950. *Courtesy of Morristown/Morris Township Free Public Library*

Broadway, Denville, 1950. Right to left: Quality Cleaners, Morristown Trust Co. Denville Supply Co. Greenwood's Drug Store, Hansa Furniture Co., Denville Public Library, delicatessen, Rodgers Insurance, Denville Theater playing "Champagne for Caesar." *Courtesy of Denville Historical Society and Museum*

Main Street, Denville, circa 1950. *Courtesy of Denville Historical Society and Museum*

In the mid 1950s travelers heading west on Route 10 in Whippany would have found its intersection with Jefferson Road much different. Before the days of "Jersey" barriers, Route 10 consisted of three lanes: eastbound, westbound and a turning lane. George Fanok's Tavern in the large building on the eastbound side was a popular stop for a drink or a bite to eat. The building still stands today across from the Hanover Township Municipal building. *Courtesy of Robert F. Krygoski*

Lake Hopatcong Yacht Club, 1955. *Courtesy of Lake Hopatcong Historical Museum*

A view of Denville center where the Key Foods is now located. At the left is the Dickerson house. The white house in center was torn down in October, 1960. *Courtesy of Denville Historical Society and Museum*

The corner of East Halsey and Parsippany Roads, circa 1960. *Courtesy of The Parsippany Historical and Preservation Society*

This mid 1950s view looking west on Route 10 in Whippany shows very few motorists. On the eastbound side you can see the Silver Anchor Restaurant, which grew into DeMaio's (which closed in the 1990s) with the Anchor Swim Club in the rear. Today this is where Route 287 passes over Route 10. *Courtesy of Robert F. Krygoski*

Street scene, Dover, 1962. *Courtesy of Lake Hopatcong Historical Museum*

Morris Plains, Speedwell Avenue looking south, 1964. *Courtesy of Morris Plains Museum Association*

Centennial Building in Chester, 1950s. This structure was built in 1876. *Courtesy of Joan S. Case*

Sunday morning on Main Street, Succasunna, 1962. *Courtesy Roxbury Township Historical Society*

West Blackwell Street, Dover, 1967.
Courtesy of Lake Hopatcong Historical Museum

Looking from railroad overpass to Madison's Main Street after a snowstorm. *Courtesy of Madison Public Library*

View of the spires in Madison, 1969. *Courtesy of Madison Historical Society*

Aerial view of Lake Hopatcong, circa 1965. *Courtesy of Lake Hopatcong Historical Museum*

This circa 1960 aerial view of Whippany looks down Route 10 towards the east. The white roofed building at the upper right is part of the Hanover Mill complex of Whippany Paper Board. Just to the right of the mill is Bell Labs. Crossing the highway at the lower right is the Morristown & Erie Railroad, whose depot, freight house, water tank and pond can be observed in the center alongside the single-track mainline. Just west of the railroad crossing is the lumberyard of Morristown Lumber & Supply Co. *Courtesy of Whippany Railroad Museum*

Downtown Madison, circa 1969. *Courtesy of Madison Historical Society*

EDUCATION

The surge in Morris County's population in the 1940s, 50s and 60s (the number of housing units more than doubled in that period) meant more families with school-aged children. Between 7 a.m. and 8 a.m., yellow school buses drove the streets of new suburbs and developments, while in the older, well-defined towns boys and girls walked to school, walked home for lunch, and then walked back to school. Many of those schools are still in use today.

In addition to studying math, English, science and French, girls took sewing and cooking. Boys took woodshop. Teachers were strict and the kids were well-behaved, if you listen to the way your mother tells it. Students learned about subjects, verbs and predicates from behind wooden desks and studied multiplication tables from the blackboard. Nary a computer or television screen was in sight.

This was before Woodstock and tie-dyed clothes and the sit-ins of the 1960s. It was before blue jeans and Walkmen and cell phones. Schoolgirls wore dresses and bobby socks. Boys wore shirts and slacks and sweaters. Boys played football, and girls were cheerleaders. Hopscotch, jump-rope, jacks and Green Light were the playground games of choice.

Those were simpler times of fewer standardized tests and fewer alternatives. In the '40s, children returned home from school (mom seldom worked and was often home waiting) and listened to The Lone Ranger on the radio. In the '50s they tuned in black-and-white television. In the '60s came stereo and color …. and a succession of teenage heartthrobs, starting with Elvis and peaking with the Beatles.

John Ehrhardt, editor of the Eagle-Courier Newspaper, visits with Deane Smith, librarian at the Children's Little Library in the James Building on Green Village Road, Madison, 1952. *Courtesy of Madison Historical Society*

Southern Boulevard School classroom, 1941. *Courtesy of Historical Society of the Township of Chatham*

School children from Southern Boulevard School, circa 1940.
Courtesy of Historical Society of the Township of Chatham

Chester Public School, eighth grade class, 1944. Charles Williamson was the teacher and principal. Those known, front row: Luella Thornton, Elanore Nass, Jean Leck, Evelyn Stroud, Elvira Filiberto, Alice Dunn, Clem Robinson, Joyce Gray Wyckoff, Jeannie Cowie Forsythe and Phyliss Furrier. Back row: Charles Williamson, Fred Shann, Billy Seals, Eddie Kappas, Herman Rademacher, Walter Conklin, Harry Emmons, Donald Romeline and Ray Crott. *Courtesy of Joan S. Case*

Denville School, eighth grade graduating class, 1940. *Courtesy of Denville Historical Society and Museum*

Morris Plains Borough School, 8th grade class, 1943. *Courtesy of Morris Plains Museum Association*

Borough School, Morris Plains, 1947. *Courtesy of Morris Plains Museum Association*

Morris Township school buses, 1948. *Courtesy of Morristown/Morris Township Free Public Library*

Alfred Vail Jr. High School students on the school stage, 1948. Those known: Bob Simms, Alyean Redfern, Kemper Chambers, Jean Van Riper, Steward Fife and William Warrick. *Courtesy of Morristown/Morris Township Free Public Library*

Morristown High School undefeated, state championship football team of 1948. *Courtesy of Morristown/Morris Township Free Public Library*

Morris Township school board members, 1948. Those known: Dr. Fergus Tufts, Sheldon Bennett, Francis DelMonico, Douglas Wiss, Dr. Robinson and Francis Westbrook. *Courtesy of Morristown/Morris Township Free Public Library*

Green Avenue School, which was built in 1879, Madison. *Courtesy of Madison Public Library*

Morris Plains classroom, 1949. *Courtesy of Morris Plains Museum Association*

Borough School classroom, 1948. Miss Madeline Glaab (later, Mrs. Carleton Bruen) addresses her class of fourth graders. *Courtesy of Morris Plains Museum Association*

Madison High School golf team, state golf champions in 1951, which defeated all the other schools, public and private in New Jersey. In the photo: Ryer Schermerhorn, Tony LoSapio, Patsy Palma, coach Koehler, Jim Cabler, Fred Iossa and Bill Carroll.

Courtesy of Madison Historical Society

On April 5, 1951, "Kumrovec Day," Chester school children brought gifts of pencils, erasers, pads and pictures of themselves to send home with a visiting deligation from Kumrovec, Yugoslavia. This photo, taken during the program, includes from left, Milton Emmons, William Cowie, Arnold Nichols and Kimber McWilliams. *Courtesy of Joan S. Case*

Safety patrol in front of Thomas Jefferson School, Morristown, circa 1954. *Courtesy of Morristown/Morris Township Free Public Library*

Netcong High School, circa 1955. *Courtesy of Thea Dunkle, Mt. Olive Township Historical Society*

In 1956, the Madison Majorettes adopted the new name the "Dodgerettes." The Dodgerettes performed at football games, school concerts and parades. The squad was made up of head Dodgerette Pat Jagger, Betty Abraham, Betsey Baker, Lois Cox, Joan Pallitto, Gloria Rakoczy and Carol Swartz. *Courtesy of Madison Historical Society*

Protesting the dismissal of Dean Ranson at Drew University, Madison, January, 1967. *Courtesy of Madison Historical Society*

Southern Boulevard School students in the reading corner, November 1959. Left to right: Mike Leander, Clark Beam, Miss Margaret Belcher, Jerry Doolittle, Patty Conlan and Lois Prudden. *Courtesy of Historical Society of the Township of Chatham*

Girls archery team at Madison High School, 1964. *Courtesy of Madison Historical Society*

Drew University demonstration, Madison, 1967. *Courtesy of Madison Historical Society*

Chair-making demonstration at what is believed to be The Seeing Eye, Morris Township, 1969. *Courtesy of Morristown/Morris Township Free Public Library, Parker Studio.*

Sewing demonstration at what is believed to be The Seeing Eye, Morris Township, 1969. *Courtesy of Morristown/Morris Township Free Public Library, Parker Studio*

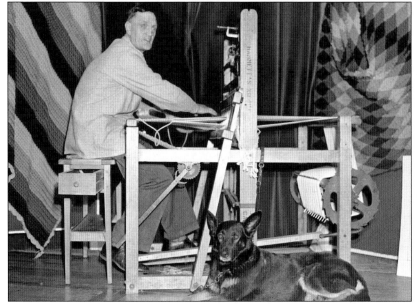

Weaving demonstration at what is believed to be The Seeing Eye, Morris Township, 1969. *Courtesy of Morristown/Morris Township Free Public Library, Parker Studio*

School girls dressed-up in 1870s clothing during a program at Washington Valley Schoolhouse, 1969. *Courtesy of Morristown/Morris Township Free Public Library, Parker Studio*

The Littleton School House, Parsippany, circa 1960. *Courtesy of The Parsippany Historical and Preservation Society*

St. Elizabeth College Convent, Florham Park. *Courtesy of Morristown/Morris Township Free Public Library*

Madison High School on Ridge-dale Avenue, circa 1969. *Courtesy of Madison Public Library*

Rear view of Washington Valley Schoolhouse with archeologist Edward S. Rutsch who was demonstrating a dig, 1969. *Courtesy of Morristown/Morris Township Free Public Library*

Archeologist Edward S. Rutsch at a demonstration dig at the Washington Valley Schoolhouse, 1969. *Courtesy of Morristown/Morris Township Free Public Library*

COMMERCE & INDUSTRY

In Morris County, more money and more people meant more commerce. By 1970, Morris County had the fourth highest per capita income among New Jersey counties – $5,318. (The median household income in the 2000 Census was put at $82,422, and incomes in Morris were among the highest in the nation.) From 1940 to 1969, the population had grown an astounding 205 percent, to 383,454, the fastest of any county in New Jersey and the fastest of any decades in the 20th century. More and more people were escaping from New York, and elsewhere, and Morris County had the jobs for them.

Accompanying the growth was the post-World War II movement of corporate headquarters out of New York. Warner-Lambert and Allied (later to become AlliedSignal, and then Honeywell) led the way to Morris County. They were accompanied by others, and the area was soon to become home for large office parks and a center of the state's telecommunications and pharmaceutical industries.

The look and feel of things changed. Life became faster, more congested. Routes 80 and 287 crossed the county, bringing motorists, homeowners and businesses. Chatham Township, after a five-year construction ban during World War II, was invaded by home-hungry families as large farms gave way to luxurious homesites. Former rose farms became major shopping centers at a corner known as Hickory Tree, named for a hickory tree planted during President Madison's term. Madison, the rose city, which once supplied the flowers to New York, was soon to become better known as a nice place to live.

The retail and service sectors of the local economy grew, too. Small mom-and-pop businesses were still the mainstay, but that was changing. Bamberger's, the big department store that would later become Macy's, moved to Morristown's shopping district, dominating the small stores around the Green. The county's first big enclosed mall, Rockaway Townsquare, wasn't even a dream yet, but it would come soon.

The Daily Record in Morristown, circa 1940.   *Courtesy of Morristown/Morris Township Free Public Library*

Johnson's Storage Co., Morristown, circa 1940. *Courtesy of Morristown/Morris Township Free Public Library*

First National Bank, Morristown, 1940. *Courtesy of Morristown/Morris Township Free Public Library*

Original Harry's Store at Fairmount Avenue and Meyersville Road, Chatham Township, circa 1940. *Courtesy of Historical Society of the Township of Chatham*

Bamberger's department store, Morristown, circa 1950. *Courtesy of Morristown/Morris Township Free Public Library*

Morristown businesses, Speedwell Avenue, circa 1940. *Courtesy of Morristown/Morris Township Free Public Library*

Businesses at Elm and South streets, Morristown, circa 1940.
Courtesy of Morristown/Morris Township Free Public Library

Lake Parsippany Inn on Parsippany Road, Lake Parsippany, circa 1940. *Courtesy of The Parsippany Historical and Preservation Society*

Louis Heyl and Arthur Heyl Sr., the first two of four generations of rose growers, Green Village, 1940s. *Courtesy of Historical Society of the Township of Chatham*

Giordano Bros. store owners, circa 1940. Left to right: James, Frank Jr. and Joseph.
Courtesy of Morristown/Morris Township Free Public Library

Giordano Bros. store, Morristown, circa 1940. *Courtesy of Morristown/Morris Township Free Public Library*

City bus crashes through Giordano Bros. store on Spring Street, Morristown, October 31, 1961. *Courtesy of Morristown/Morris Township Free Public Library*

Lyon's Movie Theater on Lincoln Place, Madison, was built in 1925. Photo, circa 1940. *Courtesy of Madison Public Library*

Madison Hardware delivery truck, circa 1940. *Courtesy of Madison Public Library*

The Women's Club of Morristown, located on South Street. Also in the photo is the sign for the Hotel Revere, which was located on South Street at Community Place, circa 1940. *Courtesy of Morristown/Morris Township Free Public Library*

Noe Farm milk truck, circa 1940. *Courtesy of Madison Public Library*

Farmhouse built by Issac Corwin about 1800. In 1829, James Topping bought it for $1,400, and in the 1940s Willis Larison purchased the property and turned it into Larison's Turkey Farm, the landmark restaurant that it is today. *Courtesy of Joan S. Case*

Joe Layer Jr., 1941. For 67 years, the Joseph Layer Butcher Shop existed in Morris Plains, despite being burned out twice. The younger Layer closed the store for the last time in 1962. Joe Layer Jr. and his wife, Adelaide, were civic-minded and served their town in many way throughout the years. *Courtesy of Morris Plains Museum Association*

Chester Oil Co., circa 1940. This company sold wholesale fuel oils, gasoline, and kerosene and was located at the intersection of Routes 206 and 24. *Courtesy of Joan S. Case*

Original Silk City Diner, manufactured in Paterson, located on Route 46 in Ledgewood in 1942. Still in use today. *Courtesy Roxbury Township Historical Society*

Davis Drugs, Morristown, circa 1946. *Courtesy of Morristown/Morris Township Free Public Library*

Rose City Garage and Rose City Stand store at 247 Main Street, Madison, circa 1940. *Courtesy of Madison Public Library*

Pfizer, Inc. in Parsippany, circa 1949.
Courtesy of The Parsippany Historical and Preservation Society

Charlie Ohto, Ray Ketch, Allan DeSombre and John Verki (manager) in the meat section of the A&P Supermarket on Main Street, Madison, 1940s.

Courtesy of Madison Public Library

Schneck, Price, Smith and King Law Firm employees and spouses at a 30-year anniversary celebration, circa 1942. Top row, left to right: Ed Vogt, Luther Stryker, Ben White, Edna Vogt, Elvira Caray, Lucy Young, Edmund Hays, C. Stanley Smith, Mary Jamison, Florance LeFurge, Hattie Loree, Eliza Garabant and unidentified. Bottom row: Judge Harold Price, Robert Schenck, Carl Vogt, Elmer King, Rosemary Kelly, Elmer S. King, Dorothy Shapiro, Chalton Price and Mildred Logan.

Courtesy of Morristown/Morris Township Free Public Library

George Washington Coffee Refining Co. was established in Brooklyn in 1909 with financial support from Warner Sugar Inc. Washington discovered the process for producing instant coffee, and his company produced soluble coffee. It became a large business during World War I since soluble coffee was part of standard infantry rations. In 1927, a new plant was built in Morris Plains, and he relocated his entire company. In 1943, Washington retired at age 72 and sold his plant to American Home Foods Inc. During World War II, about 300 women worked in the packaging department. Photo, 1940s. *Courtesy of Morris Plains Museum Association*

Business district, Netcong, 1940s. *Courtesy of Thea Dunkle, Mt. Olive Township Historical Society*

Central Lunch and Restaurant, Dover, 1940s. *Courtesy of Lake Hopatcong Historical Museum*

Flormanns' Hardware, Denville, circa 1946. Photo by Paul Flormann, *Courtesy of Denville Historical Society and Museum*

Watchung Rose Corp., summer, 1947.
Courtesy of Historical Society of the Township of Chatham

Bottle Hill Tavern, February 1, 1947.
Courtesy of Madison Historical Society

Madison Diner with Goumas home in the back at 95 Main Street, Madison. The diner was opened in 1926 by Stefanos Goumas and burned down in 1960. It became the site of the Nautilus Diner. *Courtesy of Madison Public Library*

A later photo of the Madison Diner after extensive remodeling. *Courtesy of Madison Public Library*

Harry Harootunian hands out mail at Harry's Store, 1940s. *Courtesy of Historical Society of the Township of Chatham*

Wigwam Restaurant, Budd Lake, 1940s. *Courtesy of Thea Dunkle, Mt. Olive Township Historical Society*

Barnes Bros. Marina, Mt. Arlington, on Lake Hopatcong, circa 1950. *Courtesy of Lake Hopatcong Historical Museum*

Cerbo Farm produce stand at 430 Littleton Road, Parsippany, circa 1954. *Courtesy of The Parsippany Historical and Preservation Society*

The Inn, Budd Lake, circa 1950. *Courtesy of Thea Dunkle, Mt. Olive Township Historical Society*

Eden Mill as seen from Eden Mill Lane in Whippany, June 1957, while the complex was undergoing a $24 million expansion by the Whippany Paper Board Co. Note the hundreds of waste paper bales stored outside awaiting processing. This mill ceased operating in 1980 and was razed during the 1990s. *Courtesy of Anthony Russomano; Whippany Railway Museum Collection*

Morris Plains Drive-In Theatre, circa 1950. *Courtesy of Thea Dunkle, Mt. Olive Township Historical Society*

Madison Pet Shop. *Courtesy of Madison Historical Society*

On December 27, 1927, the First National Bank of Whippany was created by 13 local businessmen. Today the bank building, nearly double its original size, remains at the intersection of Route 10 West and Whippany Road. In the background of this February 1962 snowy scene, up on the hill to the right, can be seen the outline of the 1913-era Whippany School. *Courtesy of Anthony Russomano; Whippany Railway Museum Collection*

Schwartz Dairy Farm truck, 1950s. *Courtesy of Historical Society of the Township of Chatham*

Employees inside the Stop and Shop Market, Denville, 1950. Left to right: Frank Stargo, Evelyn Heider, Pa Wershing, Gus Loven, unidentified, Ruth Meehan, Louise Post and Clarence Drake. *Courtesy of Denville Historical Society and Museum*

The Stop and Shop Market at 67 Bloomfield Avenue, Denville, circa 1950. This building was a skating rink from 1961-1969, then Bonds Ice Cream Store and most recently, Hunan Restaurant. *Courtesy of Denville Historical Society and Museum*

Budd Lake Garage, 1950s. *Courtesy of Thea Dunkle, Mt. Olive Township Historical Society*

Three Sisters Restaurant in Dover, 1950s. *Courtesy of Lake Hopatcong Historical Society*

Schenck, Price, Smith and King law firm employees., circa 1952. Top row, left to right: Charles Buck, Leonard Segal, David Cohn, Clifford Starrett, Richard Thomas, John Lee, Donald Bedell, Francis Beyrent, William Albrecht, Robert W. King, Garret Hobart, Alton Read, Robert McNabb and Richard Steffan. Bottom row: Ed Vogt, Harold Price, Robert Schenck, Elmer S. King and Ben D. White. *Courtesy of Morristown/Morris Township Free Public Library*

Howe Plant Market at 201 Main Street, Madison, 1952. It later became J&M Florists.
Courtesy of Madison Historical Society

Lynn Pancoast and Ken Haynes in the advertising office of the Eagle-Courier newspaper, 1952. *Courtesy of Madison Historical Society*

Alfred's Sport Shop. *Courtesy of Madison Historical Society*

The Stony Brook Mill's administration building, as well as a portion of the working plant, in the Malapardis section of Whippany in March 1957. In the late 1890s an earlier incarnation of this mill was purchased by the McEwan Brothers and became their principal box-making plant. In 1945, Stony Brook was acquired by the Desidero Brothers' Whippany Paper Board Co. The mill was finally shut down in the late 1970s and dismantled in the early 1980s.
Courtesy of Anthony Russomano; Whippany Railway Museum Collection

L.M. Noe Estate Greenhouses (10 in all), L.A. Noe Range on right (14 in all), Louis Noe's house in the middle of the photo, J.L Doremus house at extreme left, Jack Noe's house at, extreme right, and three workmen cottages near the greenhouse, 1950s. *Courtesy of Historical Society of the Township of Chatham*

Palace Theater in Netcong, 1950s. *Courtesy of Lake Hopatcong Historical Museum*

Flower shop at Ruzicka Greenhouses, May 1952. *Courtesy of Madison Historical Society*

Cement block plant off Summit Avenue, Chatham, 1952. *Courtesy of Madison Historical Society*

Travelers Diner, Route 46, Dover, circa 1960. *Courtesy of Lake Hopatcong Historical Museum*

Although the giant smoke stack spells out "McEwan Bros.," by the time this photo was taken on July 4, 1955, Eden Mill in Whippany had been under the ownership of the Desiderio Brothers' Whippany Paper Board Co. for 10 years. The Morristown & Erie's mainline is located alongside the complex. *Courtesy of Thomas T. Taber III; Whippany Railway Museum Collection*

This aerial view shows Whippany Paper Board's giant Eden Mill complex after it was enlarged and modernized in 1958 at a cost of $24 million. By 1959, this facility, at one time the largest paper mill in the northeastern U.S., was in full operation with a daily capacity of nearly 1,000 tons of paperboard. The shipping room at Eden was large enough to house 20 railroad boxcars and 29 trailer trucks under one roof. The mill shut down in August 1980 and was dismantled in the 1990s. *Courtesy collection of Steven Hepler*

J.J. Newberry's department store, Dover, late 1950s. *Courtesy of Lake Hopatcong Historical Museum*

Foerster's Greenhouse, July 25, 1960, stood on Route 46 in Denville, near where Route 80 now crosses. *Courtesy of Denville Historical Society and Museum*

Parks Fruit Farm produce stand, Chester, 1960s. In 1906, William F. Parks purchased this farm, mainly as a dairy farm, but he also planted apple and peach trees. *Courtesy of Joan S. Case*

Pete's Snack Bar, Shore Hills, Landing, in the 1950s. *Courtesy of Lake Hopatcong Historical Museum*

King Canal Store and Homestead, Ledgewood, 1964. *Courtesy Roxbury Township Historical Society*

Bottle Hill Restaurant opening as The Widow Brown's Inn, July, 1967. *Courtesy of Madison Historical Society*

Whippany Paper Board's Stony Brook Mill, located off Route 10 West and Jefferson Road in Whippany, produced about 150 tons of paperboard daily. Of the two 8-cylinder board units, No. 1 turned out approximately 60 tons per day of set-up and folding box board, while No. 2 had a capacity of 90 tons of tube stock used in the making of paper board cores, set-up and folding boxboard, lightweight chipboards and certain specialty grades. Stony Brook was one of four Whippany mills contributing to a record production of 389,802 tons of paper product in 1960. *Courtesy of Whippany Railway Museum Collection*

Three Sisters Restaurant, Dover, 1960s. *Courtesy of Lake Hopatcong Historical Museum*

The falls of the Whippany River at Hanover Dam near the intersection of Route 10 East and Whippany Road in Whippany, March 1957. In the background is the rear of the International Paper Co. on Parsippany Road. *Courtesy of Anthony Russomano; Whippany Railway Museum Collection*

Modern paper making machinery being installed at the Whippany Paper Board Co. Eden Mill at Whippany, in 1958 during at $24 million upgrade of the plant. *Courtesy of Anthony Russomano; Whippany Railway Museum Collection*

MORRISTOWN DAILY RECORD

Morris County's Daily for Morris County Readers

FINAL EDITION

THE WEATHER
Today — cloudy, high, and temperature; tonight — cloudy, not much change in temperature; tomorrow — cloudy, followed by clearing and colder.

VOL. XLII. No. 140.   FOURTEEN PAGES.   MORRISTOWN, N. J., MONDAY, DECEMBER 8, 1941.   MEMBER OF THE ASSOCIATED PRESS   PRICE THREE CENTS

Congress Quickly Votes War

82-0 In Senate; Woman Only Opposition In House

Japs Cause Much Damage

Congress Shows Greatest Unity In Unprecedented Speed On War Resolution

WASHINGTON (AP)—The text of President Roosevelt's war message to Congress follows:

Navy Admits Warship, Destroyer Lost
—FDR Reports 1500 Dead In Hawaii
—Several Jap Planes And Subs Sunk

County Already On War Footing

Japs Claim Big Victory

Churchill Declares War On Japan

Latest News Of War With Japan

U.S. Pacific Fleet Remains At Sea

Text Of President's War Message

War Resolution Text

WEATHER
SHOWERS TONIGHT
COLDER TOMORROW

DAILY RECORD
MORRIS COUNTY'S

AVERAGE DAILY PAID CIRCULATION IN OCTOBER
24,727
4,221 over October '62

LXIV—NO. 129   2742 BY THE MORRISTOWN DAILY RECORD, INC.   MORRISTOWN, N. J.   SATURDAY, NOVEMBER 23, 1963.   Tel. JE 8-2000   HOME FINAL EDITION   PRICE SEVEN CENTS

Johnson Takes Over Helm Of Grieving United States

Return Body Of J.F. Kennedy To White House

By CARL P. LEUBSDORF

World Mourns Death Of John F. Kennedy

WASHINGTON (AP)—Asking God's help, Lyndon B. Johnson gathered up the monumental problems of the presidency today as the world, the nation and his family mourned John F. Kennedy, dead by an assassin's bullets.

Casket holding the body of the late President rests on a catafalque in the center of the East Room.

Lee Harvey Oswald

Charged With Gun Slaying

Over 60 Die In Fire

IN MEMORIAM

TO OUR LATE PRESIDENT

Churchill

DINNER DANCE

Inside The Record

PICTURE PAGE, assassination related photos, Page 2
COUNTY RESIDENTS SHOCKED, Page 17
EDITORIAL COMMENT, local, national, Page 4
PICTURE OF OSWALD, Page 2

PROCLAMATION
JOHN B. BICKFORD

TRANSPORTATION

The interstate highway system would have a profound impact on railroading. In fact, a large portion of the Delaware Lackawanna & Western Railroad's Boonton Line east of Morris County was lost to the construction of Route 80, which crosses the county on its way west from New York.

Another major impact came with the diesel locomotive. Although diesel switchers entered the Lackawanna roster in 1926, steam engines retained a major presence until the mid-1940s. But by the summer of 1953, steam was at the end of the road. On the Morristown & Erie, which linked Morristown with the Erie Railroad in Essex Fells, the last steam engines were scrapped in 1955. Steam locomotives were relegated to historic preservation railroads – like the Morris County Central, which began operating on Morristown & Erie tracks in 1965 – and museums.

Much of the freight traveling between the New York metropolitan area and the Poconos, Midwest and beyond traveled through Morris County. The Boonton Line had favorable grades as compared to the railroad's Morris & Essex Line, where most of the commuter service was located. The Morristown & Erie was successful getting many industries to locate along its 11-mile line.

The engineering marvel known as the Lackawanna Cutoff, a shortcut to Pennsylvania starting in Roxbury, was heavily used even after financial difficulties forced the Erie and DL&W to form the Erie Lackawanna in the early 1960s.

After World War II, long-distance passenger travel began a steady decline. The varnish on the DL&W, including the famous Phoebe Snow from Hoboken to Buffalo, would fade away.

Morristown & Erie engine No. 12 works the Whippany yard on November 27, 1946. Brakeman Ken Jones rides the footboards as the train rumbles past a maintenance shanty and the Whippany Station. The M&E purchased this locomotive second-hand from the Monongahela Railway in Pennsylvania just five months prior to the photograph. The engine was built in 1912 by the American Locomotive Co. *Courtesy of Donald Van Court: Whippany Railway Museum Collection*

Morristown & Erie locomotive fireman Jerry Miller fills Engine No. 9's tender with water from the Whippany tank during the summer of 1940. One year later, Miller would suffer a fatal hear attack at this same location. *Courtesy of Whippany Railway Museum Collection*

Morristown & Erie locomotive engineer Thomas Meslar was known for stopping his train to allow automobiles to cross the tracks. Meslar began his railroad career with M&E predecessor Whippany River Railroad in July 1895. He eventually became a locomotive fireman. When he retired as engineer on August 15, 1945, he had 50 years of service with the railroad. *Courtesy collection of Steven Hepler*

A 1935 Ford parked in front of the Madison Post Office. *Courtesy of Madison Public Library*

Infamous Ledgewood Traffic Circle at Route 46 and Route 10, Roxbury, 1940.
Courtesy Roxbury Township Historical Society

Delaware, Lackawanna & Western Railroad steam locomotive No. 1612, rated at 70 mph, is seen thundering through Denville in 1948 over the Boonton Line with a long freight out of Port Morris, bound for Hoboken. Built by the American Locomotive Co. in 1929, these magnificent 1600-class locomotives were named "Pocono"-types, in honor of the mountainous terrain they conquered. *Courtesy of John Maris, Sr.; Whippany Railway Museum Collection*

On April 11, 1960, a raging fire destroyed the Morristown & Erie's archaic wooden enginehouse at Morristown. Firefighters arrived and fought the blaze, but they were unable to save the structure. M&E diesel locomotive No. 14 was trapped inside the building, but, damage was confined to burned electrical wiring and a ruined paint job. The locomotive was shipped back to builder American Locomotive in Schenectady, N.Y. for repairs. *Courtesy of Morristown & Erie Railroad; Collection of Steven Hepler*

The day after the enginehouse fire, a pitiful looking No. 14 sits outside the scorched remains of her former home. The Morristown & Erie eventually tore down the building and replaced it with a modern, two-track metal structure that is still in use today as the railroad's maintenance facility and general office. *Courtesy of Whippany Railway Museum Collection*

A driver attempts to guide his automobile through the sagging tree limbs on Greenwood Avenue at Dodge Field (looking north) during a sleet storm in 1948. *Courtesy of Madison Public Library*

Morristown & Erie engine No. 9 backs a short train across the three-lane Newark & Mt. Pleasant Turnpike (present-day Route 10) in Whippany on November 16, 1942. The crew is shuttling the cars back to the McEwan Brothers Paper Box Board plant (Eden Mill). *Courtesy of Donald Van Court; Whippany Railway Museum Collection*

An early motorized scooter is this young man's transportation choice, Chatham Township. *Courtesy of Historical Society of the Township of Chatham*

At the end of a long workday maintaining the roadbed, the Morristown & Erie's track gang places Motor Car No. 3 back in its shed at Morristown on April 8, 1942. *Courtesy of Donald Van Court; Whippany Railway Museum Collection*

The Morristown & Erie's maintenance gang stops at Thomas Street (present-day Parsippany Road) in Whippany with Motor Car No. 4 February 25, 1943. From left to right are: John Farrinhotto, Joe Dandino and Frank Studley. *Courtesy of Donald Van Court; Whippany Railway Museum Collection*

The Morristown & Erie Railroad entered the diesel era on April 28, 1952. On that day, brand-new diesel No. 14 arrived at Whippany on its first trip. The engine was built by the American Locomotive Co. and was rated at 1,000 horsepower. Standing in front of the locomotive are, from left to right: Henry E. Becker, director; Phil Dahill, roundhouse foreman; Mauritius Jensen, vice-president; Richard W. McEwan Jr., president; Joe Danino, brakeman; Tommy Gee, conductor; Howard Roff, engineer; Ken Jones, fireman; Frank Studley, brakeman; and Fletcher Williams, superintendent. The locomotive was named in honor of Jensen, who had been with the railroad for 50 years.

Courtesy of Whippany Railway Museum Collection

Commuter parking lot on the corner of King's Road and Prospect Street, Madison, 1948.

Courtesy of Madison Public Library

Morristown & Erie's track gang in the early 1960s. From left to right, Theodore "T.D." Davis, David Morgan, Frank McKenna, Benjamin "Billy Goat" Eggleston and Harold "Willie" Sandure (foreman). In the front center is Gilbert "Shorty" Watson.

Courtesy of Morristown & Erie Railroad; Collection of Steven Hepler

Morris County Central Railroad locomotive No. 385 makes its way east out of Whippany and crosses the School Street bridge on a scheduled run in 1967. In the background is Whippany School, located on Highland Avenue. *Courtesy of Edwill H. Brown; Whippany Railway Museum Collection*

Intertstate 80, May 1966. *Courtesy Daily Record archives*

Construction of Route 80 through Parsippany, March 28, 1968. *Courtesy Daily Record archives*

Construction of the Route 80 exit onto Route 46, Denville, February 1969. *Courtesy Daily Record archives*

In November 1967, Morris County Central locomotive No. 4039 teamed with MCC engine No. 385 at Whippany prior to the start of a special excursion over the Morristown & Erie to Essex Fells. Built in November 1942 by the American Locomotive Co. No. 4039 made its final trip under steam in 1980. Now owned by the Whippany Railway Museum, 4039 has been awarded a federal grant that will see it return to active service again. In March of 2002, No. 4039 was recognized as a National Treasure when she was listed on the National Register of Historic Places by the U.S. Department of the Interior. *Courtesy collection of Steven Hepler*

Morristown & Erie Railroad General Manager Arthur B. Vreeland is seated at his rolltop desk at Whippany Station in September 1962. Starting as a clerk in 1927, he worked his way up through the offices of the railroad. After his service in the military during World War II, he returned to become auditor. Vreeland was one of the last of the old-time M&E employees and was loved and respected by many in the company. *Courtesy of Whippany Railway Museum Collection*

Morris County Central excursion locomotive Nos. 4039 and 385 climb the grade eastbound between Ridgedale Avenue (in the background) and DeForrest Avenue in East Hanover on November 6, 1966. The two engines were leading a special doubleheaded run to Roseland to celebrate No. 385's 59th year. *Courtesy collection of Steven Hepler*

One day after diesel No. 14 made its first run over the Morristown & Erie, Mauritius Jensen posed on the gangway at Whippany on April 29, 1952, when the new locomotive was named in his honor. On that day, M&E president Richard W. McEwan Jr. paid tribute to Jensen's faithful service as company auditor, vice-president and secretary. *Courtesy of Whippany Railway Museum Collection*

Steam Locomotive No. 4039 rolls across the Ridgedale Avenue grade crossing in East Hanover in April 1967, nearly a year after being overhauled and placed in passenger excursion service by the Morris County Central Railroad. This historic locomotive is now owned by the Whippany Railway Museum and holds the title as "The Official Steam Locomotive of Morris County." *Courtesy of Edwill H. Brown, Whippany Railway Museum Collection*

The general office staff of the Morristown & Erie Railroad in front of the Whippany Station on September 13, 1955. From left to right are: Jeanette Anderson, car accountant; Thomas Peterson, assistant agent; Fletcher Williams, superintendent; and Margaret Dooling, bookkeeper. *Courtesy of Thomas T. Taber, III; Whippany Railway Museum Collection*

Morristown & Erie vice-president Mauritius Jensen (left) and M&E president Richard W. McEwan Jr. at Whippany Station in the early 1950s. Jensen "retired" at age 70 on October 1, 1945, but he continued to act as the railroad's vice-president until his death at age 90 in 1966. He had given more than 50 years of service to the M&E. *Courtesy of Thomas T. Taber, III; Whippany Railway Museum Collection*

Aerial view of Route 287 construction showing the Franklin Street Bridge near Jefferson Avenue, August 5, 1968. *Courtesy Daily Record archives*

The new iron beams (above) that will be the new Madison Avenue/Route 24 bridge across Route 287, January 29, 1969. The bridge in the background is Franklin Street. youngsters skate in what will be the northbound lanes of Route 287. *Courtesy Daily Record archives*

Route 287 construction in Morristown, looking west, January 25, 1969. *Courtesy Daily Record archives*

Madison Avenue detour near Jefferson Avenue during Route 287 construction, November 16, 1968. *Courtesy Daily Record archives*

HOME & FARM

If you lived in Chatham Township in the 1940s, you might have greeted the morning with a bowl of berries dressed with fresh cream from nearby Anderson dairy farm. Those were the days when Franklin D. Roosevelt and Harry Truman sat in the White House, cows were still being milked and hay was harvested throughout Morris County. It was a time of fewer people and many fewer highways.

If you were rich, the strawberries could have been the start of a full English breakfast of farm eggs and bacon, served to you in your multistory mansion. But these were the final days of the huge houses built for the wealthy financiers and industrialists of New York, some of whom managed a life of high society through the Great Depression, World War II and the longest bear market in history. The introduction of the income tax, rising property taxes and higher living costs put an end to that style of living and to the private ownership of many of the great houses of Morris County.

The Frelinghuysens, a locally-famous family of senators and congressmen, gave up Whippany Farm, with its Colonial-revival style mansion built in 1891, and its 127 acres. Now it is home to the Morris County Park Commission and hosts thousands of flower lovers as Frelinghuysen Arboretum. The F. W. Bienecke family donated their Madison mansion, acquired in 1925, to Drew University in 1949. In the same year, Morristown resident and philanthropist W. Parsons Todd acquired Macculloch Hall from the Macculloch-Miller family to display his collection of 18th and 19th century American and English fine and decorative arts.

Most of the mansions of the era are gone, turned into commercial or professional buildings, or the property of historical or preservation societies. Virtually all the farmland has been given over to residential development. Still, anyone who strolls down Macculloch or Maple avenues in Morristown, or drives through Chatham Township and Green Village, or goes pumpkin picking in Chester Township, will not find it too hard to picture the homes and farms of yesteryear.

Heber Cushing Peter's residence, Budd Lake. Mr. Peter built and owned the Casino and Wigwam, popular Budd Lake attractions. *Courtesy of Thea Dunkle, Mt. Olive Township Historical Society*

Revere House, DeHart Street, Morristown, was also Sansay Dancing School. Photo, circa 1940. *Courtesy of Morristown/Morris Township Free Public Library*

Clingen home in Long Hill (then called Passaic Township), summer, 1949. *Courtesy of Historical Society of the Township of Chatham*

Eric Anderson, owner of Anderson's Dairy, 1942, near the township of Chatham.
Courtesy of Historical Society of the Township of Chatham

George and Roberta Davidson built this home at 158 Green Avenue in 1910. In 1925, F. W. Bienecke acquired it and donated the home to Drew University in 1949. *Courtesy of Madison Historical Society*

Macculloch Hall, Morristown, in the 1960s, before renovations. *Courtesy of Morristown/ Morris Township Free Public Library*

Pulling hay wagon on the Anderson property, Southern Boulevard, 1946. *Courtesy of Historical Society of the Township of Chatham*

Silas Riggs Salt Box house on its original site on East Main Street, Ledgewood before move in 1962. *Courtesy Roxbury Township Historical Society*

Silas Riggs salt box house under restoration at new site 1967. *Courtesy Roxbury Township Historical Society*

Silas Riggs salt box house on moving day as it crosses Route No. 10 to its new site on West Main Street, Ledgewood, 1962. *Courtesy Roxbury Township Historical Society*

Legend has it that this oven (one of three) owned by Ellis Cook and later James Burnet, was where bread was baked for George Washington's soldiers. The house was located at the corner of Park and Ridgedale avenues. *Courtesy of Madison Historical Society*

Legendary house owned by Ellis Cook and later James Burnet was demolished in 1963. *Courtesy of Madison Historical Society*

Whippany Farm, former home of George G. and Sarah Ballentine Frelinghuysen, was bequeathed to the Morris County Park Commission in 1969. This colonial revival house now serves as the park commission's headquarters. *Courtesy of Morristown/Morris Township Free Public Library*

SOCIETY

Participants at a 1968 civil rights rally in Madison probably would have been surprised to see it followed, 33 years later, by a court-protected rally in Morristown led by a white supremacist. For decades, towns of Morris County have been the center of all types of religious, civic and political activity.

Life after World War II still revolved around work, society, family and church. The Rotary Club, the Elks Lodge, the Conservation Club, the Women's Club and the Garden Club were fixtures everywhere. Few women held jobs outside the home, but that hardly meant they sat about idly. Instead they could be seen kneeling in knee-length skirts to plant trees to shade the streets of Madison or organizing a flea market to raise money for the local YMCA.

A post-war construction boom in Chatham Township, Madison, Morristown and the surrounding towns saw farmland replaced by single-family housing. The population of New Jersey as a whole shifted from being 18.4 percent rural in 1940 to 11.1 percent rural in 1970, and the population in Morris County grew at rates never seen before or since. Churches and synagogues saw rapid growth. Enthusiasm for civic ventures and civic organizations, like Rotary and garden clubs, was high. In 1964, the Morristown Garden Club celebrated its 50th anniversary.

With shopping centers starting to develop in the late '60s and malls not far away, the area was suburbanizing faster than nearly anyone imagined. It wouldn't be long before Morris County bore little resemblance to the small town America of its forefathers.

The Jewish Center in Morristown. *Courtesy of Morristown/Morris Township Free Public Library*

Mt. Kemble Home, Mt. Kemble Avenue, Morristown, circa 1940. *Courtesy of Morristown/Morris Township Free Public Library*

Green Village Methodist Church, 1940s. *Courtesy of Historical Society of the Township of Chatham*

Undenominational Church was formed in 1929. The cornerstone reads November 17, 1940. *Courtesy of Denville Historical Society and Museum*

South Street Presbyterian Church, Morristown, 1942. *Courtesy of Morris County Historical Society*

A.C. Rockefeller Band played at many Chester functions. Photo, 1940s. Seated: Joe (on the drums), Dorothy (on the piano), Elizabeth (on the guitar) and Della (on the mandolin). Standing: Arthur Jr. (on the trumpet) Arthur Sr. (on the violin), Charles (on the sax) and George (on the banjo). *Courtesy of Joan S. Case*

Chatham Art Club, 1941. Those known, left to right: Albert Bross, John Moomaw, Delight Rushmore and Philbrick Crouch. *Courtesy of Historical Society of the Township of Chatham*

Group of Chester folks in front of Lon Green's pharmacy, circa 1944. The two gentlemen seated in the center are Bill Smith, left, and John Rockefeller. The two women pictured at right are Mae Scheld (in the hat) and Caroline Smalley. On the far left, leaning against the post is Gordon Barker. The boy on the bike is Walt Conklin, and the woman on the steps is Ada Myers, with her little brother Henry. The man seated on the first step is Doug Fleming. Burt Masker sits with his dog "Zombie." The older gentleman sitting on the far left of the bench is Sam Ammerman. *Courtesy of Joan S. Case.*

First Presbyterian Church, Dover, 1940s. The church was erected 1899-1901 and dedicated in 1901. *Courtesy of Morristown/Morris Township Free Public Library*

Wedding day photo for Gilbert and Louella Watson pictured in the front row, second and third from the left, 1946. James Gregory, first African-American policeman in Morristown is in the second row, second from the left. Also included in the photo: Alberta Peterson, Anabelle Monroe, Robert Preston, John Watson, Jr., Clara W. Pinkman, "Boscoe" Robinson, Quintin Davis, Mary W. Robinson, Francie Watson and Rosetta Coleman. *Courtesy of Morristown/ Morris Township Free Public Library*

Red Cross meeting at the Red Brick Schoolhouse, 1940s. *Courtesy of Historical Society of the Township of Chatham*

Percy Steel, first president of the Morris County Urban League, and Thomas Sprinell (right), 1940s. *Courtesy of Morristown/Morris Township Free Public Library*

Girl Scouts participate in a World War II War bond rally, Roxbury, 1940s. *Courtesy Roxbury Township Historical Society*

Morristown Rotary Club, 1940s. *Courtesy of Morristown/Morris Township Free Public Library*

First Presbyterian Church (Hilltop), Mendham. *Courtesy of Thea Dunkle, Mt. Olive Township Historical Society*

Morristown Elks Lodge members. Those known, bottom row: Ken Marshall, Harry Marks, Bill Ryerson, Carl B. Scherzer, chairman of trustees. Top row: Jim Howie, Jack Rayder, Joe Hand. *Courtesy of Morris County Historical Society*

Relaxing at Lake Hiawatha, Summer of 1948. *Courtesy of The Parsippany Historical and Preservation Society*

Interior of the First Congregational Church of Chester, built in 1856. This is an example of perhaps one of the two remaining "trompe l'oeil" decorations in the state. *Courtesy of Joan Case*

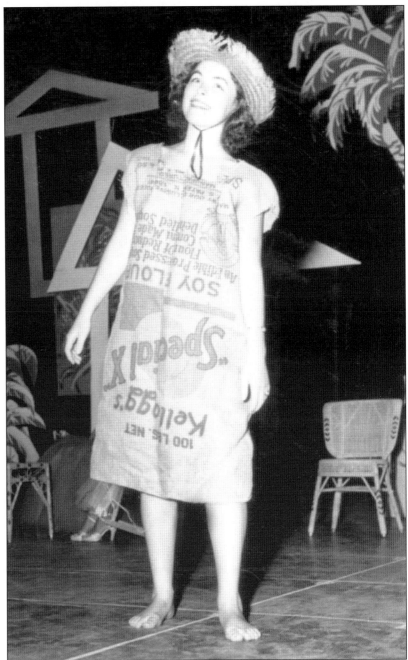

Joanne McClay, Miss Lake Hopatcong contestant in the 1953 Miss New Jersey pageant. *Courtesy of Lake Hopatcong Historical Museum*

Members of the Fairmount Woman's Club in front of the historic Chatham Schoolhouse, May 16, 1954. Pictured are: Margaret Gabrielson, president; Dorothy Newsome, former president; and Eleanor Faller. *Courtesy of Historical Society of the Township of Chatham*

Morristown Garden Club members celebrate the 50th anniversary of their organization, circa 1964. In the photo: Anne Dunbar, Etta Larsen, Marie Halsted, Carolyn Foster. *Courtesy of Morristown/Morris Township Free Public Library*

Grand opening of the Madison Area YMCA, February 10, 1963. The ground-breaking ceremony was held August 6, 1961. *Courtesy of Madison Historical Society*

Union Hill Presbyterian Church congregation, Denville, 1963. *Courtesy of Denville Historical Society and Museum*

Janet Adams, Miss Lake Hopatcong, who later became Miss New Jersey in 1963, competing in Atlantic City. She had a successful 25-year career on stage and is a minister in California today. *Courtesy of Lake Hopatcong Historical Museum*

John Pinkman, Vic Wiss and Gordon Parsons at the doorway of St. Peter's Episcopal Church on South Street, Morristown. *Courtesy of Morristown/Morris Township Free Public Library*

Organizers of the Madison Area YMCA Flea Mart, April 1964. *Courtesy of Madison Historical Society*

Drew students picket in Madison, May 1964. An incident occurred when Somalian Ali Hasson Dulai was refused service in a barbershop in downtown Madison. In a separate incident a few days later, two local African-Americans, Thomas P. Sellers Jr. of Madison (whose wife, Frances, was a respected manager at Drew University for many years) and Reginald Barrow, walked into Philip Gatti's barbershop and were likewise turned away. From these separate incidents arose a landmark New Jersey case that ended blatant racial discrimination in services licensed and controlled as a public accommodation by the state. Drew students, faculty and Madison citizens also spearheaded protests against the barbers. *Courtesy of Madison Historical Society*

The bar mitzvah of Will and Miriam Cogen's son Matthew at the first Lake Hiawatha Jewish Center. From 1942 until 1945, religious services were conducted be Rabbi joseph Schreiber in his home at 156 North Beverwyck Road. In 1945, the first Lake Hiawatha Jewish Center opened on the corner of Nokomis Avenue and Lake Hiawatha Boulevard. Rabbi Sam Mendelowitz became the first full-time rabbi of the congregation. In 1964, a new synagogue was erected on Lincoln Avenue.

Courtesy of The Parsippany Historical and Preservation Society

Civil rights rally at the College of St. Elizabeth at Convent Station, Madison, May, 1968. *Courtesy of Madison Historical Society*

Dedication of Community Park, 1964. Paul Bangiola and Dr. Robert McLeod lower the time capsule. *Courtesy of Morris Plains Museum Association*

Bethel AME Church, Morristown, circa 1969.
Courtesy of Morristown/Morris Township Free Public Library

Presbyterian Church, Madison.
Courtesy of Madison Historical Society

Construction of Temple B'Nai Or in Morristown. *Courtesy of Morristown/Morris Township Free Public Library*

RECREATION

It was the lakes and the wide open greenery that made Morris County different, a summer haven for the rich from New York, a welcome respite for city folk from the dog days of August. The railroads opened the lakes and the surrounding hills and mountains to everyone, and by mid-century they were popular destinations for homeowners and daytrippers alike. Lake Hopatcong, the granddaddy of them all, drew thousands, especially to Bertand Island, where a big waterfront amusement park offered fast rides, clean-water swimming and a carefree day away from home. Kids and their parents flocked there … and elsewhere, too – to Budd Lake, Lee's Park, Lake Musconetcong, Indian Lake and dozens of other attractions. World War II soldiers convalesced on their shores. Motorboats plied the waters. Visitors stayed in cabins. Thousands built homes.

There were the usual small-town pasttimes on land, too – baseball, softball, Soap Box Derby contests, double features at the movies with Bing Crosby and Dick Powell. And there was Morris County's nascent park system. In the mid 1950s it consisted of nothing. By 1982 the county had acquired more than 7,500 acres, many donated, and the park system is now considered among the state's best. One of the most popular places in Morris County to hike, bike and get away from it all is the Great Swamp, which in 1959 was targeted by the Port Authority of New York as the site of a huge new metropolitan jetport. Local citizens rose to fight the plan. Led by Marcellus Hartley Dodge, who gave 1,000 acres in the swamp to the North American Wildlife Foundation, they won: In 1968 Congress passed a law designating the swamp a national wildlife refuge. Now on any given weekend you can find hundreds of people there quietly watching for hawks, cycling down quiet roads and having, in the most densely populated state in the nation, an out-of-the-house experience.

George "Butch" Prudden with a wagonful of puppies at Dodge Field, 1948. *Courtesy of Madison Public Library*

A friendly game of horseshoes at Indian Lake, Denville, circa 1940. *Courtesy of Morristown/Morris Township Free Public Library*

Sun-worshippers enjoying a sunny day at Indian Lake, Denville, circa 1940. *Courtesy of Morristown/Morris Township Free Public Library*

Boating on Lake Hopatcong, circa 1940. These boats were made by Barnes Brothers of Lake Hopatcong. *Courtesy of Lake Hopatcong Historical Museum*

World War II soldiers with their family and friends at Lake Hopatcong, 1940s.

Courtesy of Morristown/Morris Township Free Public Library

Balloon blowing contest at Union Hill Field Day, 1940.

Courtesy of Denville Historical Society and Museum

World War II soldiers with their family and friends at Lake Hopatcong, 1940s.

Courtesy of Morristown/Morris Township Free Public Library

Diving and swimming at Lake Parsippany, 1941. *Courtesy of The Parsippany Historical and Preservation Society*

Airport Inn Lake Hopatcong baseball team, 1950s *Courtesy of Lake Hopatcong Historical Museum*

Alan Florin, 1940s, future mayor of Morris Plains, tries out a soapbox car, built at his father's service station on Speedwell Avenue near Five Corners.
Courtesy of Morris Plains Museum Association

First annual softball banquet, Green Village, 1946. *Courtesy of Historical Society of the Township of Chatham*

Sign announcing a Fourth of July victory parade and celebration in Chester, 1940s. *Courtesy of Joan S. Case*

Campers at Camp Morris, Mt. Olive, 1948. *Courtesy of Morris County Historical Society*

Lois "Tommy" Barker, of Chester played for the Grand Rapids Chicks in 1950. Phil Wrigley, owner of the Chicago Cubs, decided people needed some sort of recreation when men were in the service and gas was being rationed. Lois is listed in Baseball's Hall of Fame. *Courtesy of Joan S. Case*

Swimming at Camp Morris, Mt. Olive, 1948. *Courtesy of Morris County Historical Society*

Children with their pets at Dodge Field, 1948. The only person identified is Helene Chamberlain with her goldfish.
Courtesy of Madison Public Library

Soapbox Derby on Maple Avenue, Madison, late 1940s. Those known: Jim Bradley, Tom Douglass, Mrs. Denardo, Jimmy Testa, Donald Lacy, Teddy Pennington and Bob Fredrickson.
Courtesy of Madison Historical Society

Morris Plains Girls Sports Club members, 1950. Left to right, front row: Shirley Stewart, Dona Scoble Hausser, Carla Capuano, June Meeker Peterson, Jane Wilhelm and Shirley Hansen Ford. Middle row: Kathryn Youngs Elgood, Pat Cullen Dorflinger, Jackie Gorry Markey, Helen Myers Dower, Joyce Heinhold and Rita Kapinos Brown. Back row: Sue Gorry Edwards, Jim McIntyre (coach), and Doris Campbell Riddle. *Courtesy of Morris Plains Museum Association*

Morris Plains Boys Sports Club Baseball Team with coach and manager Bill Backes, 1950. Back row: Dick Henderson, Walter Olin, Harry Hansen, Leon Knauer, Bill Howell and Bill Backes. Front row: Allen Bertholf, Bob Backes, Rick Sofield, Don Backes and Russ Edmonds. *Courtesy of Morris Plains Museum Association*

Merry-go-round at Budd Lake, circa 1950. *Courtesy of Thea Dunkle, Mt. Olive Township Historical Society*

Brick cabins one mile east of Budd Lake, circa 1950. *Courtesy of Thea Dunkle, Mt. Olive Township Historical Society*

New Jersey Vasa Home, Budd Lake, late 1940s. *Courtesy of Thea Dunkle, Mt. Olive Township Historical Society*

New Jersey Vasa Home, circa 1950. This is a view of the terrace adjoining the club house and swimming pool. *Courtesy of Thea Dunkle, Mt. Olive Township Historical Society*

Bertrand Island Park promotional photo with Allen Cuda, grandson of the founder of the park, and Evelyn Craney, daughter of one of the people who had a stand at the park, 1958. *Courtesy of Lake Hopatcong Historical Museum*

Swimming at Lake Musconetcong. *Courtesy of Joan Case*

Bertrand Island Park promotional photo with Allen Cuda and Evelyn Craney, 1958.
Courtesy of Lake Hopatcong Historical Museum

Budd Lake and Route 6 (now 46), 1950s. *Courtesy of Thea Dunkle, Mt. Olive Township Historical Society*

Scandinavian tradition at Vasa Park, Budd Lake, 1950s. *Courtesy of Thea Dunkle, Mt. Olive Township Historical Society*

Lee's Park in Mt. Arlington. *Courtesy of Lake Hopatcong Historical Museum*

Aero Jet ride at Bertrand Island Park. Three space ships 20 feet long swung over the lake. *Courtesy of Lake Hopatcong Historical Museum*

Fountain at Hopatcong State Park 1960. *Courtesy Roxbury Township Historical Society*

Beach at Bertrand Island Park with the Aero Jet ride and the carousel house in the background. The park closed on Labor Day 1983. *Courtesy of Lake Hopatcong Historical Museum*

Lake Musconetcong dam and State Park Beach was a beautiful place for recreation, circa 1965. *Courtesy of Thea Dunkle, Mt. Olive Township Historical Society*

Budd Lake was a popular place to cool off in the summertime, 1950s. *Courtesy of Thea Dunkle, Mt. Olive Township Historical Society*

Boating on Budd Lake, late 1960s. *Courtesy of Thea Dunkle, Mt. Olive Township Historical Society*

Beach bathers at Budd Lake, late 1960s. *Courtesy of Thea Dunkle, Mt. Olive Township Historical Society*

Boaters at Budd Lake, late 1960s. *Courtesy of Thea Dunkle, Mt. Olive Township Historical Society*

George Forsythe raced this car with his brother Charlie at Flemington Speedway. His wife, Lil, owned this coffee shop in Chester.

Courtesy of Joan S. Case

PUBLIC SERVICE

Some served at the town fire department, which were all volunteer, as most still are today. Others ran for elective office in towns and county governments that were nearly all male (things are different today), all white, and predominantly GOP. And thousands went off to fight in World War II, gathering first for those ceremonial photos outside town halls, then shipping out for training and to warships and battlefields overseas. They were there at Omaha Beach. Some recall Pearl Harbor. Thousands never came back. Those who did came back heroes and more than 50 years later many received Distinguished Service Medals from Morris County.

Even those who stayed home volunteered, working for the Red Cross and the hospitals and all the other causes of the day, and filling the jobs vacated by those who went to war. Thousands went to Picatinny Arsenal, the Army weapons and research development center outside Dover where cannonballs were made for the Revolutionary War. At its peak in the 1940s, 18,000 civilians worked there making ammunition we used against the Germans and Japanese. By the end of the century employment was less than 4,000, and although Picatinny still did important work developing new weapons and shells, its future seemed less certain than at nearly any time in the past.

Women also served the community in more traditional ways. They organized the fundraising to preserve historic houses and staff newly opened museums. They were the driving force behind the social, cultural and aesthetic development of the booming towns. And garden clubs and women's clubs sprang up in every community.

Morristown Fire Department, Engine Co. No. 2, circa 1940. On the engine is Joe De Groat and George E. Peters. *Courtesy of Morristown/Morris Township Free Public Library*

Morris County Courthouse, 1941. *Courtesy of Morristown/Morris Township Free Public Library*

Palma House fire, Madison, March 9, 1941. Firemen are: R. Vanderhoof, E. Daniher Jr., R. Mackenzie, E. Diemer, C. Earles. *Courtesy of Madison Historical Society*

A 1941 Dodge fire engine in front of the Green Village Volunteer Fire Company, May 18, 1963. *Courtesy of Historical Society of the Township of Chatham*

Morristown Fire Department, 1942. *Courtesy of Morristown/Morris Township Free Public Library*

The Rockaway Neck Fire Company, circa 1940. Left to right, front row: Richard Klepp and Former Mayor Francis X. Downey. Back row: Steve Giercyk, Ralph Stecker, Red Lands, Horace Green, Carl Levitt, Walter Coddington, Kent Dixon, and Charlie Coddington. Standing next to the flag is William Wood. *Courtesy of The Parsippany Historical and Preservation Society*

The Women's Auxiliary of the Rockaway Neck Fire Company, circa 1940. *Courtesy of The Parsippany Historical and Preservation Society*

Munitions plant at Picatinny Arsenal during World War II. *Courtesy of Lake Hopatcong Historical Museum*

Soldier in front of his car, 1943, Denville. The movie marquee in the background has playing "Rhythm on the River" with Bing Crosby and "I Want A Divorce" with Dick Powell. *Courtesy of Denville Historical Society and Museum*

Denville Fire Department inspection, 1944. Left to right, front row: George Keeffe, Albert Vialard, James Lash, Edward Doremus, Adelbert Doremus, William Green (seated), Robert Ronan, Fred Jagger, Burl Cook, Horace Cook. Second row: George Scott, Charles Salle, George Herzog, James Beatty, Arthur Hopler, Mathew Casey, William Cullen, William Stevens, William Champion, William Keeffe. Back row: Joseph Lash, Lloyd Shannan, John Morgan, Alfred Bowe, Edgar Armstrong, Robert Ranft, Stanley Peer, Harry Hulit, James Gallagher. *Courtesy of Denville Historical Society and Museum*

First group of World War II inductees, Borough Hall, January 12, 1942. *Courtesy of Madison Historical Society*

Munitions at Picatinny Arsenal during World War II. *Courtesy Lake Hopatcong Historical Museum*

In 1944, many years after this photo was taken at her family home, Jean "Bunny" Osborne would become the first woman parcel post carrier in New Jersey. Later she became Morris Plains tax collector, another all-male domain. *Courtesy of Morris Plains Museum Association*

Denville Police officers Chief Jenkins, Sam Gill, Jack Kelly and Arthur Strathman, August 17, 1947. *Courtesy of Denville Historical Society and Museum*

Mount Olive Municipal Building, Budd Lake, 1940. *Courtesy of Thea Dunkle, Mt. Olive Township Historical Society*

Edward Barry, the first full-time police officer in Morris Plains, 1940s. *Courtesy of Morris Plains Museum Association*

Chester Ladies Auxiliary, July 4, 1949. Left to right: Sara Sliker, Lulu O'Dell, Anna Williamson, Madeline Steinberg, Muriel Blaine, Mrs. Buldger Blaine, Beatrice Wyckoff Case, Greta Nunn and three unknown. *Courtesy of Joan S. Case*

Municipal Building, built in 1942, Morris Plains. It replaced an old wooden structure destroyed by fire in 1940 and served both the fire department and local
government. *Courtesy of Morris Plains Museum Association*

Morris Plains Police Chief Edward Barry next to a car in front of the municipal
building. *Courtesy of Morris Plains Museum Association*

Livingston Building fire on East Blackwell Street, Dover, March 28, 1948. Rockaway Borough, Wharton, Denville and Randolph No. 2 were called to extinguish
the fire. *Courtesy of Morris County Historical Society*

Denville Fire Department, 1950.
*Courtesy of Denville Historical Society
and Museum*

City officials in the basement of the old firehouse, Denville. Left to right: Harry Jenkins, Doc Gould, Bill Green, William Keffee Sr., Mayor Hogan, Fred Jagger, Mr. Ulit and Phil Crowther. *Photo by Paul Flormann, Courtesy of Denville Historical Society and Museum*

Morris County Freeholders, 1950. *Courtesy of Morris County Historical Society*

Denville Township Committee, 1950. *Courtesy of Denville Historical Society and Museum*

Members of the Chester first aid squad and the fire department, 1951. Those known, front row: Arnold Martenis, Paul Sutton, Reuben Thompson, George McFarren, Walt Patrie, Kenneth O'Dell, Herman Clausen and Herman Rademacher. Middle row: Warren Kay, Gert Dean, Millie Barkman, Art Lee, Irvin Tredway, Leroy "Shorty" Nunn and Charlie Williamson. Back row: Emile Ardin, Tom Dean, Lee Case, Jack Hoffman and Al O'Brien.

Courtesy of Joan S. Case

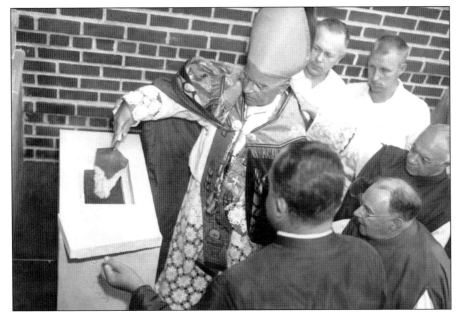

Bishop laying the cornerstone of St. Clare's Hospital, Denville, August 31, 1952.

Courtesy of Denville Historical Society and Museum

The U. S. Post Office in Chester, 1950s. *Courtesy of Joan S. Case*

Wayside Inn fire, Denville, January 1953. *Courtesy of Denville Historical Society and Museum*

Morristown firemen, circa 1954. *Courtesy of Morristown/Morris Township Free Public Library*

Parsippany Civil Defense Police Auxiliary in 1956. *Courtesy of The Parsippany Historical and Preservation Society*

Charter firemen Albert Lindstrom, Stanley H. Lyon and Frank Gilligan, with the department's first piece of equipment, the hand pumper, Morris Plains, 1957. *Courtesy of Morris Plains Museum Association*

Chatham Township emergency workers, 1961. *Courtesy of Historical Society of the Township of Chatham*

Morris County Courthouse, January 15, 1966. *Courtesy of Morristown/Morris Township Free Public Library*

The Annual Inspection day for the Whippany Fire Department, circa 1955, brings out all the members. Those known, front row: Jack O'Donnell (fire commissioner), Al Steele, Ed Guerin, William Polhemus, John Tibus, George Pillion, Frank Krygoski, Bill Fakler, Bob Griffith, Chief Ted Guerin, John Kasiski (fire commissioner). Back row: Bob Kasiski, Joe Lopata, unknown, unknown, Bill Lopata, George Welshko, Andy Lopata, Tony Yavorski, Andy Maher, George Minto, Dick Japko, Rudy Adamsky, Charlie Coughlen, Ed Makowski, unknown, unknown, Dick Glackin. *Courtesy of Robert F. Krygoski*

Chief George Burns rides a white stallion, Morris Plains, 1963. As a joke, Dr. James Weisert, the chief organizer of the 1963 Memorial Day parade, spread the rumor that the chief of police would lead the parade on a white stallion. Chief Burns, who had extensive riding experience, actually did lead the parade on this stallion. *Courtesy of Morris Plains Museum Association*

New Roxbury Town Hall and police headquarters as well as new and old fire engines, 1950. *Courtesy Roxbury Township Historical Society*

Special officers of the Hanover Township Police Department, mid 1950s. They volunteered to patrol the township with a full-time paid officer and helped assist with traffic at large gatherings. Standing from left to right are Bill Kreck, Joe Misko, Ken Hagen, Harry Bennett, unknown. Sitting is Elvin Henderson. *Courtesy of Robert F. Krygoski*

Morristown Fire Department, F.M.B.A. Local 43, 1964. Left to right, front row: John Timpson, Angelo Cacchio, Stephen France, Chief Francis Geary, Dep. Chief George Nixon, Norman Brown, William Franey and Albert Hopping. Back row: Ellsworth Pruden, Edward Cavanaugh, Austin Caulfield, Martin Mackin, Vincent Galligan, Le Roy Brown, George Sullivan, William Amerman, Albert Norton and Richard Isel. Missing Robert Evans and Joe Ellias. *Courtesy of Morristown/Morris Township Free Public Library*

One of Madison's worst fires, Pomeroy Road, 1966. *Courtesy of Madison Historical Society*

Morris Plains Town Council, 1967. Left to right: William Dobbing, Carl Lerman, Harold Baglin, Paul Bangiola, Mayor Pete Rudden, Adalaide Layer (town clerk), Jim McErlane, John Armitage, Joe Sellitto and Charles Paron. *Courtesy of Morris Plains Museum Association*

CELEBRATION

How little we've changed. Parades 50 years ago were a lot like parades now: lots of stiff-suited, flat hatted firemen and majorettes, lots of high school marching bands, and lots of American flags. There were the politicians, of course, dressed up and marching proud. In Chester a Fourth of July parade featured horses … and the young men of the Aircraft Warning Service. In 1951 Morris Plains celebrated its 25th year of separation from Hanover Township with a parade. Madison celebrated its tercentenary with a parade and floats 13 years later. Santa returned to Morristown that December, as he does every year, not so much with a parade, but with an arrival for hundreds of expectant children. And each Memorial Day one town after another more quietly celebrated the sacrifices of dead American servicemen.

Parades haven't changed (except there are more fire engines these days). Just the people and outfits have.

Denville Memorial Day Parade down Main Street, 1940. *Courtesy of Denville Historical Society and Museum*

Marching around the Green, in Morristown, 1940.
Courtesy of Morristown/Morris Township Free Public Library

July 4, 1942, parade in Morristown. *Courtesy of Morristown/Morris Township Free Public Library*

Fourth of July celebration, Morristown, 1941. The float "My Sister and I" was created by the Morristown Business & Professional Women's Club. Mrs. Grace Harquail, Miss Mary E. McWhinney, Kathleen Harquail and Raymond Harquail. *Courtesy of Morristown/Morris Township Free Public Library*

Memorial Day parade, early 1940s, featuring the Madison Bugle & Drum Corps, organized in 1939. *Courtesy of Madison Public Library*

Memorial Day parade in Madison, early 1940s. *Courtesy of Madison Public Library*

"The Rose City" float in the Morris County Centennial parade, 1940s. *Courtesy of Madison Public Library*

Parade celebrating the 75th anniversary of the Dover Volunteer Fire Department, July 4, 1949. *Courtesy of Morris County Historical Society*

Old fire pumper in a Chester parade, 1947. Reuben Thompson has the reins, and the man on the back is Jack Hoffman. The third man is unidentified. *Courtesy of Joan S. Case*

Chester parade along Main Street by the old post office and Chester House, circa 1950. *Courtesy of Joan S. Case*

Red Cross marching in Chester, circa 1950. *Courtesy of Joan S. Case*

Post 216B Aircraft Warning Service men from Chester in a Fourth of July parade along Main Street, circa 1950. Clinton Mack and Joseph Croot hold the sign. Dudley Bragg, unidentified, Paul Apgar and Tom Dean are in the second row. *Courtesy Joan S. Case*

Gay Nineties party, Lake Hopatcong Yacht Club, August 26, 1950. *Courtesy of Lake Hopatcong Historical Museum*

Horseback riders during a Chester parade, circa 1950. They are coming up Grove Street, alongside a French restaurant. *Courtesy of Joan S. Case*

Crowds watch as Santa arrives in Morristown, December 10, 1951. *Courtesy of Morristown/Morris Township Free Public Library*

Horse pull at the county fair, Parsippany, 1950s. *Courtesy of Morristown/Morris Township Free Public Library*

Morris Plains celebrates 25 years of independence from Hanover Township on the steps of the borough hall, June 1951. *Courtesy of Morris Plains Museum Association*

Edward Barry, chief of police, marches in the Morris Plains 25th anniversary parade, 1951. He was the first full-time Morris Plains policeman with formal police training. *Courtesy of Morris Plains Museum Association*

Barbara Wikander, Vera Craig and her sister pose as "Faith, Hope, and Charity" on a float constructed by Emil Possi and Carl Ahlfield for the 1951 anniversary parade in Morris Plains. *Courtesy of Morris Plains Museum Association*

Gerald Coursen (mayor), Milt Trompen (councilman), Fred Reeves (councilman), Herbert Ueltz (borough clerk) and Griff Humphrey (councilman) march in the 1951 Morris Plains parade. They are in front of the 200-year-old Young-Clark building on the corner of Jaqui Avenue. *Courtesy of Morris Plains Museum Association*

Annual Holiday Parade, early 1960s, on Broadway, Denville. *Courtesy of Denville Historical Society and Museum*

Memorial Day Parade, 1964. Madison High School Band led by Mayor William G. Nordling. *Courtesy of Madison Public Library*

Denville parade down Main Street, 1950s. *Paul Flormann photo, Courtesy of Denville Historical Society and Museum*

Whippany Fire Department members in a 1958 Memorial Day Parade. In the color guard are, left to right: Dick Japko, Jack Kasiski, John Keena, Joe Lopata. Center: Chief Ted Guerin. Right column: Frank Krygoski, John Krygoski, John Zailo, Andy Lopata, Bob Kasiski. Left column: Dick Glackin, Bob Keenan, Mike Yavorski. *Courtesy of Robert F. Krygoski*

FINIS

MORRISTOWN DAILY RECORD
Morris County's Daily for Morris County Readers

VOL. XLVI — NO. 43.   TWELVE PAGES.   MORRISTOWN, N. J., WEDNESDAY, AUGUST 15, 1945.   PRICE THREE CENTS

Weather: Today scattered showers. Tonight and tomorrow clear, cooler, low humidity.

Nation Enjoying 2-Day Holiday Celebrating Ending Of Jap War

Staid Morristown Goes Wild As News Of Victory Comes

Observance Of 2-Day Holiday Very General

All Manpower Curbs Ended With Hiring Made Local

Japanese To Be Under Control Of MacArthur

JAPS' BOSS—GENERAL MacARTHUR

How Emperor Hirohito Broke Precedent And Gave News To Japanese People

Peace Terms Reduce Japan To '95 Status

Six Men Arraigned After Free-For-All

Edge Proclaims 2-Day Holiday

China, Reds Sign Treaty

False Alarm

Hit By Shot During Dover Celebration

240 Jamaicans To Be Relieved From Picatinny

Meys Tells Of County Boys Enjoying Record At Sea

OPA Lifts Ration Ban On Gas, Fuel Oil, Cans

CHURCH SERVICES

WM. C. HURTZIG, Inc.
Fire Insurance
Tel. Mo. 4-2700

KIWANIS CLUB

Chamber of Commerce entry, Tercentenary Parade, Madison. *Courtesy of Madison Historical Society*

Madison Fire Department during the Tercentenary parade. *Courtesy of Madison Historical Society*